Fundamentals

A simple guide to Catholicism

Thank you to everyone who helped me with this book.

Richard Harrison

Contents

Introduction

Introduction

This book is meant to be a basic introduction to Catholicism. It is aimed at simply explaining some of the core beliefs and rules in being a modern day Catholic. The Catholic Church is the one and only true Church of Jesus Christ. If a church is not in communion* with the Catholic church it simply does not correctly worship and follow Jesus.

By no way is this an apologetics book or an all-encompassing guide to the Catholic church or Faith. I am just a humble convert, nobody special just one of God's children, who wishes to try his best at spreading the one true Faith. I wrote this small book in the hope it helps. This type of book I believe would have really helped me on my journey many years ago and so I tried with my limited skill to write it. I have written this book to be small in size and easy to read, it will not go into very much depth on any subject I cover. This is to make it more accessible and practical to use. I hope this book can be used as an on hand source to help Catholics in their lives. It will include prayers, which will help you in everyday life, as well as in more specific situations. There will be a guide to the Rosary and the Mysteries, which is a vital spiritual tool. There will be information on aspects of the precepts, sins and virtues as well as on Confession which is a very important part of a Catholic life. I will also offer key information on some of the core beliefs of the faithful, this I hope will offer insight for would be converts, Catholics that have let their faith diminish, people who wish to learn more about Catholicism and as a reminder for faithful Catholics, of our beliefs. There will be a reading list near the end of this book, with books and sources which I believe will help you to understand more about the faith. The reading list is designed to grow your faith and knowledge, as well as to give more details to the subjects that I have started in this book. I hope Catholics in good standing, which means Catholics that follow the Faith with their mind, heart and soul and that stay true to the Scripture, Tradition, Sacraments, Magisterium, can be charitable with this humble and simple book.

Jesus said to Peter, Mt 16:15-19,

"But what about you?" he asked. "Who do you say I am?" Simon Peter answered, "You are the Messiah, the Son of the living God." Jesus replied, "Blessed are you, Simon son of Jonah, for this was not revealed to you by flesh and blood, but by my Father in Heaven. And I tell you that you are Peter, and on this Rock, I will build my church, and the gates of Hades will not overcome it. I will give you the keys of the Kingdom of Heaven; whatever you bind on earth will be bound in Heaven, and whatever you loose on earth will be loosed in Heaven."

Key Information

Key Information

Sins and Virtues

Based on the seven deadly sins and their matching virtues.

Virtue	**Sin**
Chastity	Lust
Temperance	Gluttony
Charity	Greed
Diligence	Sloth
Patience	Wrath
Kindness	Envy
Humility	Pride

Mortal and Venial Sins.

A mortal sin is of a grave matter and requires, full awareness and knowledge of the sin, as well as for it to be done deliberately with complete consent. It causes separation from God and eternal damnation if left unrepented.

A venial sin is a lesser sin that does not cause a complete separation from God and eternal damnation, it injures your relationship with God, leading you into greater sin if unchecked.

Sins that cry out for vengeance.

Murder: homicide, abortion, infanticide, fratricide, patricide, and matricide

Sodomy: unnatural sex.

Oppression of the poor.

The taking advantage of and defrauding workers.

Virtues

A virtue is a trait or quality that is morally good and is at the core of a good moral person. It shows that an individual has high moral standards, in doing what is right and avoiding sin.

The moral virtues are acquired by practice and habit. Theology distinguishes acquired moral virtues and infused moral virtues. Catholic moral theology also holds that the theological virtues are different from the cardinal virtues, as they cannot be obtained by human effort but are infused by God into a person. Like the cardinal virtues, an individual who exercises these virtues strengthens and increases them, they are more disposed to practice them.

Theological virtues

Faith It is a gratuitous gift of God.

Hope Its opposite is the sin of despair.

Charity Its opposite is Lack of love which may give place to hatred, wrath or indifference.

The Four Cardinal virtues

Prudence also considered Wisdom the ability to discern the appropriate course of action to be taken in a given situation at the appropriate time.

Justice also considered as fairness the Greek word also having the meaning righteousness.

Fortitude also termed courage, forbearance, strength, endurance, and the ability to confront fear, uncertainty, and intimidation.

Temperance also known as restraint, the practice of self-control, abstention, discretion, and moderation tempering the appetite.

Precepts

These are six rules that help guide every Catholic, these five below are from the Catechism.

1. ("You shall attend Mass on Sundays and holy days of obligation and rest from servile labour") requires the faithful to go to mass in a church every Sunday as well as other specific days of the year. You should also rest and avoid working on these days as well.

2. ("You shall confess your [serious] sins at least once a year") You should try to confess any sin you commit as soon as possible if it is a Mortal sin.

3. ("You shall receive the sacrament of the Eucharist at least once during the Easter season") You should try to take

the Eucharist more often if your soul is clean of sins.

4. ("You shall observe the days of fasting and abstinence established by the Church") ensures the times of penance which prepare us for the liturgical feasts and help us acquire discipline over our heart.

5. ("You shall help to provide for the needs of the Church") This means donating money or time to your local church. The amount according to your own ability.

6. (You shall observe the laws of the Church concerning marriage.) Not to marry without the blessing of the Church.

Sacraments

The Sacraments give grace to the person who receives them, there are seven Sacraments, Baptism, Confirmation, Penance, Holy Eucharist, Matrimony, Holy order, Anointing of the sick.

Baptism cleanses us from original sin and makes us Catholics and children of God.

Confirmation is when you receive the Holy Spirit, to strengthen us as Catholics.

Eucharist is when you take the true body and blood of Jesus Christ, to gain grace and honour him.

Penance is when you receive forgiveness for your sins that you have committed.

Anointing the sick/ extreme unction is when a person close to death is given strength, comfort, remission from sins.

Holy Orders is when a person is given power and grace to perform sacred duties in the name of God.

Matrimony is when a special grace for the marriage is given, and it sanctifies the covenant/groom and bride themselves.

What the differences in unbelievers are.

This list is in the Baltimore Catechism #3, Lesson 30, Question 1170.

Atheists - Who deny there is a God.

Deists - Who admit there is a God but deny that He revealed a religion.

Agnostics - Who will neither admit nor deny the existence of God.

Infidels - Who have never been baptized, and who, through want of faith, refuse to be baptized.

Heretics - Who have been baptized Christians, but do not believe all the articles of faith.

Schismatics - Who have been baptized and believe all the articles of faith, but do not submit to the authority of the Pope.

Apostates - Who have rejected the true religion, in which they formerly believed, to join a false religion.

Rationalists and Materialists - Who believe only in material things.

Stances

Stances

Abortion

We care for all human life. Foetus' which are human beings, is simply a stage of life like baby, teenager or adult. From conception a human being has its own unique DNA. Killing a human being that is totally defenceless is a truly evil act, one human can not kill another just for convenience, subjective or emotional reasons, there is no valid reason. There are only subjective reasons for murdering a baby (abortion). Body autonomy, consciousness, reasoning and whatever other excuse are all invalid in both science and faith. Abortion is a sin and wrong in every case, life starts at conception all science states this, as does Catholic teaching.

IVF

IVF, In Vitro Fertilisation also known as assisted reproductive technology, ART. Is not allowed in the Catholic faith under any circumstances, because it is unnatural and against the natural order. The children that are produced by it are not sinful themselves and are not to be blamed for their parent's sin, they are to be loved. Most IVF results in the death of several children during the process as they pick one or a couple of children for the process and kill the rest or freeze them, usually to experiment on them later (killing them).

Assisted Suicide/Euthanasia

Life is a gift and to give it up freely is not just sad and unfortunate, it is also a sin. Ending your life is not what God wants, it is not what his church wants. Suffering is a virtue and though it may be difficult and sometimes feels impossible to endure, it is part of creation and thus life. Helping someone commit suicide is a sin for the same reasons, it is not an act of mercy but an act of violence. Allowing this trend of legalising Euthanasia will take humanity down a dark path and will always continually expand, who and why someone should be allowed to end their life, to the point where it will become state sanctioned mass murder.

Sexism

Sexism is a sin, God does not favour a sex, we are different but complementary. We both have our strengths and weaknesses; we work together to have a better life and work towards salvation. The Catholic church is not sexist, not now or ever. It is false that women cannot be educated and that they cannot work if needed or cannot express their views in their family choices as Catholics. Men should be the spiritual head and leader of the family, but not the dictators of it, their duties are to love and guide their families first above all things, providing is secondary. Men and women have their roles, and they must follow them. All Feminism is an anti-Catholic ideology, Women are uniquely protected in Catholicism.

Racism

Racism is a sin, God favours no race, to judge or treat races differently is a sin. To try and use other means to be racist is just as bad, like believing in eugenics, or trying to twist/lie about genetics. The misusing of IQ, to push the well disproven 'gap theory' is also sinful. Trying to cause conflict between races or using identity politics are also sinful. Racism is truly evil and is only used by the enemies of the faith. The church simply wants a faithful world, nothing else matters. Tribalism as it is used in the modern world to divide us is not tolerated in the Catholic church.

Douay-Rheims Bible, 2 Corinthians 5: 16

"Wherefore henceforth, we know no man according to the flesh. And if we have known Christ according to the flesh; but now we know him so no longer."

Note with verse.

"We know no man according to the flesh": That is, we consider not any man with regard to his nation, family, kindred, or other natural qualities or advantages; but only with relation to Christ, and according to the order of divine charity, in God, and for God. The apostle adds, that even with respect to Christ himself, he now no longer considers him according to the flesh, by taking a satisfaction in his being his countryman; his affection being now purified from all such earthly considerations.

Marriage/relationships

We are a Patriarchy as a religion and the family must be as well. The man must be the leader of the marriage, equality in leadership is not permitted. Even though the man is the head of the family there are still equality in being. The point of dating is not to have sex or because you are bored/lonely, it is to choose a husband or wife, so it should be given the appropriate respect it deserves. You should not have any form of sexual relations outside of marriage even though it may give you short term gratification, it will only damage your psyche and possibly even your body (disease). If a person dates or sleeps with 100 people, how is that individual supposed to settle down with only one person. They now compare their spouse with 100 other people. It can be difficult enough not to compare your spouse to friends or strangers. But having 100 other partners however short some of them were in time, will have a massive negative affect on your emotions and psyche not to mention your expectations and the way you handle yourself and your spouse in a marriage. If you divorce you cannot remarry inside the church, only as a widow (er) can you remarry. You may get an annulment if your spouse lied about certain subjects before marriage which in effect in the eyes of the church, the marriage was never valid. When choosing a partner for marriage you should chose a Catholic who is in good standing this is the main and only important requirement. You must be realistic in your choice of partner, there is no Mr or Mrs perfect. Looks fade quickly, weight piles on and money isn't important for happiness or salvation. Settling is a word used in todays dating world to give people an excuse to be selfish, cruel, destructive and to keep them single and unhappy and possible sinful. Marriage can only consist of one man and one woman. Divorce within the Church is not possible, it does allow for physical separation if you are being abused. Only a man and a woman can form an acceptable couple. Sex before marriage is a sin, as is masturbation which is always a sin, as it mimics the act of sex relations between a husband and wife and is not open to life.

Contraception

Contraception is always wrong married or not. It artificially assaults the couples' roles in a relationship, its closed off to life. It is unhealthy physically and mentally, damaging women profoundly. Sex is meant to be for procreation. You should not be sleeping with anyone except for the person you are married to. The only type of person you should be dating is someone who you think can be your spouse, this means someone that you want to have and raise children with and spend the rest of your life with. Contraception allows

for sin, it also lets someone have sexual activity with people, they are not compatible with, causing more even more risks/harm. The person who uses contraception is saying that the other person is unworthy of them.

The Trinity

The Trinity means that there is one God, but he exists in three persons. The three persons are, God the Father, God the Son (Jesus Christ), God the Holy Spirit. The three persons are distinct yet are one.

Science

Science is fully compatible with the Catholic church. Catholics came up with a large part of science. The Bible is not a science book, but a book on Humans living a faithful and fulfilling life and it offers the only way to salvation. The Catholic church tends to humanity and Its souls as well as how they live their lives. Catholics have not only been behind a huge part of the scientific advancement of mankind, but also have never hindered or stopped it. Genetics, big bang theory etc are all from Catholic priests. Sinful people try to drive a gap between science and the faith because they wish to push uncatholic ideas wrapped in pseudo-science on the world. Like relativism, nominalism, gender, identity politics and many more.

LGBTQ

Individuals who choose to be active as a member of the LGBTQ lifestyle cannot be a Catholic in good standing, which means they cannot marry, have the Eucharist or have salvation. They cannot produce life together and are against the natural order. All charity and tolerance must be given to these individuals and every effort must be made to help our struggling brothers and sisters. We must love them and not judge them, we do not hate them, we hate the sin. The choice is simply the opposite to all Catholic teachings as well as completely against all pillars of the Faith. They are not compatible in their current choice of lifestyle and should seek help to correct themselves for the sake of their souls. There is no true happiness or salvation with their choice, only empty short term gratification and shallow happiness. No matter their choice we must still love them.

Politics

Catholics should support a party/groups that support natural law, religious freedom as well as property rights, it must make morally good laws based on Catholic teachings. Socialism, Marxism, Communism, identity politics, Fascism, National Socialism (Nazism) do not offer these and is incompatible with Catholicism. So is unethical capitalism and crony capitalism. God has not told us of his preferred system for man to live by here on Earth. But keeping to Catholic Tradition and scripture as well as Catholic instruction will lead you to the right path and show you what to avoid.

The Eucharist

The Eucharist is the real and actual flesh of Jesus Christ himself. It is not symbolic; the host can appear as a wafer; it is called a miracle or transubstantiation. You must believe in this to be a Catholic and to get salvation. It should be taken on the tongue while on your knees if possible. Though not a sin not to kneel/tongue, it is tradition and is a good habit of respect and love for Christ. Do you not appreciate Christ's gift and sacrifice for us, would you not kneel in his presence? Many have died for the right to take the eucharist, do not allow pride or anything else to interfere with this great gift.

Confession

Confession is an important part of Catholic life; you must confess to a priest in order to get forgiveness for your sins. You can pray an act of contrition which will help but only a priest, through God, can forgive your sins. The priest does not forgive your sins, God does forgive your sins through the ministry of the priest. He can also help you in your struggles with sin by giving guidance. You must genuinely feel remorse for your sins and attempt to correct yourself from further sin. Some sins can become less severe if it is a habit or addiction. This should not stop you from trying to combat the sin itself. Confession regularly and thoroughly will build your virtues and your relationship with God.

Popes

The Pope is the father and priest of all Catholics, he is the leader of the Catholic faith. Only the Pope with the church can represent God and Christ on this earth. The Pope must be obeyed on all Magisterium issues. Not everything the Popes say has to be followed, only what is within the construct of the Magisterium, Canon law and within Tradition and Scripture. They can be sinful men who hold the position of Pope, this does not affect the teachings or the faith, simply pray for his conversion or his virtues to grow.

Other faiths

There is only one true religion, one true faith, which is the Holy Catholic church, you must not pray with other religions or partake in their rituals. An individual from another religion must be converted by free will or kept at arm's length and tolerated. Other faiths only cause confusion and more paths to sin and Hell. This includes new age nonsense, non-Catholic traditions and movements that are or have anti Catholic themes, teachings or actions. Praying or leaving offerings to other gods or spirits is forbidden. As is all forms of witchcraft and new age activities. The Catholic faith have nothing to learn from other faiths as we have the truth already, they must learn from the Catholic faith to have a chance to be saved.

Worship

Catholics must attend church weekly as well as on days of obligation, unless ill or for a lawful reason. Catholics do not worship Saints or Mary; we ask for intercession through them. Nor do we pray to idols. Mass is not meant to be entertaining but is meant to build your relationship with God, it is also to build your virtues. To devote yourself to God, for an average of 40 to 70 minutes at mass, it is a great gift from God. Do not treat this as an entertainment or social event, the act of attending mass is the highest part of worship to God as he is due our worship, as God is our creator it is our duty to worship him.

Catechism

The Catechism is a doctrine on how a catholic should live their life. It is supposed to be taught to all members of the Catholic church and used as a guide in life. It is a very important tool of the church and the faithful. The Didaché is considered to be the first catechism. The Roman Catechism, better known as the Catechism of the Council of Trent, published in 1566, was made to improve the lack of systematic knowledge and theological understanding of the clergy. It was formulated to give clarity, at a time when the secular world and heresies had infiltrated the clergy and caused confusion. The Catechism of the Catholic Church was released under Pope John Paul II in 1992. There have been no fundamental changes to the core of the catechism over time.

Canon Law

Canon law is the system of laws and ecclesiastical legal principles made and enforced by the hierarchical authorities of the Catholic Church, to regulate its external organization and government, to order and direct the activities of Catholics toward the mission of the Church. Canon law was the first modern Western legal system, it is also the oldest continuously functioning legal system in the West. It is formed with Divine law, natural law and human law, the constitution given by Jesus Christ to His Church and formulated by the church, in conformity with Divine law.

Scripture

Scripture is one of the several names denoting the inspired writings which make up the Old and New Testament. Scripture and Tradition are forms of Revelation from God. Scripture and Tradition combines with the Magisterium to give the complete Truth. Teachings of all three come from the Holy Spirit. Scripture and Tradition is Divinely guaranteed Truths and it is an Apostolic deposit, entrusted to the Catholic Church as its lawful administrator. As Scripture is difficult to interpret God gave humanity His Church to give His children the right path to Salvation.

Understanding the Bible

First reading the Bible in modern day English or another language, does not mean you understand the true meaning of the Bible. Without knowing the correct translations of words and terms you cannot have a chance of understanding the Bible. You then need to know what specific words/terms meant then and how they should be understood in modern times. You also need to know the context of what each part of the Bible means and what it tries to teach the reader. How it is meant to be understood. You also need to understand who the lessons/ information/criticisms are targeted at or for. You must therefore need to know about history/philosophy/language to even have a hope of understanding the bible.

That is why Jesus started the Catholic church, to help people understand himself and our faith. The Catholic church put the Bible together, Peter was the first Pope, he was one of Jesus' disciples and chosen to lead us to salvation, along with future Popes. Only the Catholic church can teach the faith. Only Catholics can understand the bible, which is not my opinion that is Jesus' will. This is why Christian pretenders, have so badly misinterpreted the Bible.

Natural Law

Natural law is a product of God's creation of all nature and things, all people are born with natural law/internal law and can understand it. It is human nature, different from man's law. To live in a manner against natural law is a grave matter and will cause confusion and an unhealthy mind, body, spirit and soul.

If people live by natural law, then they should live by the highest ideals of it. However we also have a soul which allows us to have free will. We are a higher being over all other life. We do need faith and the grace of the one True church, to reach eternal salvation and of course guide us in life.

The Magisterium

The Magisterium is the church's authority to give authentic interpretation of the Word of God, whether in its written form or in the form of Tradition. It may simply offer an idea for consideration without imposing it. It can also make a teaching infallible and bind it to the faith and the faithful, it can also range between the two as well.

Interviews, books and programmes with Priests, Bishops, Popes typically do not involve an exercise of the magisterium.

Magisterium has multiple meanings; it can refer to the authority which Jesus Christ has given to the Catholic Church. Those who exercise this teaching, the Pope and the Bishops teaching in union.

They are referred to as the Magisterium. It can belong to a particular body of teachings that have been authoritatively proclaimed, as in a written work from a Pope.

As well as these three uses. You can also hear other phrases like ordinary magisterium. This means the ordinary teaching of the Popes.

There is extraordinary magisterium, for instance when a Pope or ecumenical council, infallibly defines a truth. All other instances of Papal teaching are called ordinary.

Tradition

Sacred Tradition comes from Christ, handed down through each generation, which is how it is supposed to be handed down. Tradition stands with Scripture in forming the only deposit of the Faith. For Catholics Sacred Tradition is not in opposition to Scripture they complement each other.

Meaning to abandon Tradition is to abandon scripture and the faith. It is how the faith is taught without it for example, the Bible would not exist as it is. Tradition is the glue that holds the faith together, without it the faith will be acting against God. We write Tradition, with a capital T to mean Sacred Tradition and with a lower case t to mean customs which are not part of Divine Revelation.

Confession

Confession

Confession is highly important, to make a good confession you must be honest and willing to bare yourself completely and be ready to change your behaviours and habits. Here is one guide to making a good confession, there are many guides. Whilst making a confession what matters most is that you are thorough, honest, and remorseful. You should try to confess as soon as possible after committing a sin, but once a month is recommended. Catholics believe in four stages of penance, **Contrition**, the state of feeling remorseful. **Confession**, confess to a priest, you must be repentant and promise to change your ways. **Absolution**, released from the sin and guilt.

Satisfaction, the priest sets a task or prayers to be said in order to get penance.

An Examination of Conscience based on the Seven Deadly Sins, from Fr. Dylan James, is a good start.

Pride

Pride is the mother of all sin. It is a craving for excellence beyond what is reasonable. It makes a person hate being equal to others, and hate being less than God.

Have I refused to admit my own weaknesses?

Have I dwelt on the failings of others?

Have I judged others, in my thoughts or words?

Have I ranked myself better than others?

Have I borne hatred for another?

Have I refused to learn from others?

Have I been stubborn?

Refused to admit I was wrong?

Refused to accept that another person had a better idea?

Have I been arrogant?

Have I held others in contempt?

Have I neglected to use the talents that God has given me?

Vanity

Vanity is excessive concern about manifesting my glory before others.

Have I been overly concerned about what others think of me?

Have I allowed this to motivate my actions?

Have I lied or exaggerated to make myself look good?

Have I wasted undue time and money on clothes and appearance?

Have I been content with my lowly position, or have I resented the role that Christ asks of me?

Lust

Lust is disordered desire for sexual pleasure, isolated from its procreative and unitive purpose.

Have I viewed other people as mere sexual objects rather than as persons to be loved?

Pornography: On internet? or TV?

Impure Thoughts: Have I entertained impure thoughts?

Impure Acts: Alone, or with another?

Anger/Wrath

Anger is undue desire for vengeance - undue in cause or in amount.

Have I harboured resentment, grudges, and hatred in my thoughts?

Have I nurtured imaginary angry conversations?

Have I been slow to forgive?

Have I lost my temper?

Impatience: How have I carried my cross?

Have I been impatient with people, family, events, sufferings, sicknesses?

Covetousness/Avarice

Avarice is the excessive love of possessing things.

Have I been overly concerned about my own comfort?

Have I been resentful of my lack of money?

Have I been generous in giving? Have I given with a cheerful heart?

Have I cheated, stolen, or failed to pay my bills on time?

Have I used people for my own ends and advantage?

Have I wasted money?

Envy

Envy –is sadness at the happiness of another, Jealousy is coveting what belongs to another.

Have I envied or been jealous of the abilities, talents, ideas, good-looks, intelligence, clothes, possessions, money, friends, family, of another?

Gossip: Have I judged others in my thoughts?

Have I damaged the reputation of another person by my words, attitude, or looks?

Have I repeated accusations that might not be true?

Have I exaggerated?

Have I failed to defend the reputation of others?

Have I failed to keep secrets?

Do I despise others of different race, class or culture?

Lies: Have I lied or exaggerated?

Sloth/Apathy

Laziness, especially laziness in the things of God. Sloth is a sorrow in the face of spiritual good -it makes a person lethargic and want to do nothing.

Have I sought God above all else, or have I put other priorities ahead of him? (e.g. friendships, ambition, comfort and ease).

Have I got so caught up in the things of this world that I have forgotten God?

Have I risked losing my faith/piety by bad company, bad reading, cowardice, or pride?

Have I trusted God, especially in times of difficulty?

Have I attended Mass each and every Sunday?

Have I neglected to say my daily prayers?

Have I entertained distractions in prayer, or failed to give God due concentration in prayer or in the Mass?

(Note: Not giving God the effort he deserves in prayer is a sin, but it is not the same thing as involuntary weakness in mental distractions.)

Have I made a prayerful preparation before Mass and a good thanksgiving after Mass?

Have I received Holy Communion while in a state of serious sin?

Have I taken the Lord's name in vain? Or used other foul language?

Gluttony

Gluttony is the inordinate desire for food but also can be an excess of anything else.

Have I eaten more than I need?

To how serious an extent?

Have I spent excessive money on food?

Have I drunk alcohol excessively?

Have driven after drinking?

Have I eaten greedily and with little consideration for the presence and needs of those at table with me?

Have I given money to help the hungry?

Have I regularly practiced fasting and self-denial, especially on Fridays?

Have I always fasted an hour before receiving Holy Communion at Mass?

Prayers

Prayers

Prayers are a fundamental part of being a Catholic. You can incorporate all or some of these prayers into your daily life. Try to be in a peaceful state while praying, however in life this is not always possible, so try to concentrate on the issue and ask for Gods help. You may pray in any way you wish, hands together or not, kneeling or standing, sitting whichever makes you best able to concentrate on your prayers. Some prayers are to give thanks for specific things others are to ask for help in certain situations. Prayers are the way we communicate with God, by not praying you cut yourself off to him. Learning prays is very important, they have been given to us or made for us to better communicate with God, they focus our mind, heart and soul on the task. However simply remembering to thank God or ask for his help is important, so if you cannot remember a prayer straight away do not panic, just speak to God, in time you will learn the prayer and be able to communicate with God better. Prayers are food for the soul, would you starve yourself of food completely, no of course not so do not do so with your soul, feed it by praying, keep your soul full of love for God, keep your spirit strong and help others around you strong with your prayers it truly does make a difference.

Act of Contrition against Sin

O my God, I am heartily sorry for having offended You, and I detest all my sins because of Your just punishments, but most of all because they offend You, my God, who are all-good and deserving of all my love. I firmly resolve, with the help of Your grace, to sin no more and to avoid the near occasion of sin. Amen

Morning prayer

O Jesus, through the Immaculate Heart of Mary, I offer You my prayers, works, joys and sufferings of this day for all the intentions of Your Sacred Heart, in union with the Holy Sacrifice of the Mass throughout the world, in reparation for my sins, for the intentions of all my relatives and friends, and in particular for the intentions of the Holy Father. Amen.

Night Prayer by St. Alphonsus Liguori

Jesus Christ, my God, I adore you and I thank you for the many favours you have bestowed on me this day. I offer you my sleep and all the moments of this night, and I pray that you preserve me from sin. Therefore, I place myself in your most sacred side, and under the mantle of our Blessed Lady, my Mother. May the holy Angels assist me and keep me in peace, and may your blessing be upon me. Amen

Prayer Before Meals

Bless us, O Lord, and these your gifts which we are about to receive from your goodness. Through Christ our Lord. Amen

Prayer After Meals

We give Thee thanks, Almighty God, for all thy benefits, who lives and reigns for ever and ever. Amen

Prayer to Jesus

My Jesus, I believe that You are present in the most Blessed Sacrament. I love You above all things and I desire to receive You into my soul. Since I cannot now receive You sacramentally, come at least spiritually into my heart. I embrace You as if You were already there and unite myself wholly to You. Never permit me to be separated from You. Amen.

In Temptation Prayer

Lord, save me, or I perish. Keep me close to you by your grace, or I shall sin and fall away from you. Jesus, help me; Mary, help me; my holy Angel, watch over me. Amen

In Trouble Prayer

In all things may the most holy, the most just, and the most lovable will of God be done, praised, and exalted above all for ever. Your will be done, O Lord, your will be done. The Lord has given, the Lord has taken away; blessed be the name of the Lord. Amen

Prayer for Priests

Lord Jesus, present in the Most Blessed Sacrament, and living perpetually among us through Your Priests, grant that the words of Your Priests may be only Your words, that their gestures be only Your gestures, and that their lives be a true reflection of Your life.

Grant that they may be men who speak to God on behalf of His people and speak to His people of God.

Grant that they be courageous in service, serving the Church as she asks to be served.

Grant that they may be men who witness to eternity in our time, travelling on the paths of history in Your steps, and doing good for all.

Grant that they may be faithful to their commitments, zealous in their vocation and mission, clear mirrors of their own identity, and living the joy of the gift they have received.

We pray that Your Holy Mother, Mary, present throughout Your life, may be ever present in the life of Your Priests. Amen

The Nicene Creed

I believe in one God, the Father almighty, maker of heaven and earth, of all things visible and invisible.

I believe in one Lord Jesus Christ, the Only Begotten Son of God, born of the Father before all ages. God from God, Light from Light, true God from true God, begotten, not made, consubstantial with the Father; through him all things were made. For us men and for our salvation he came down from heaven, and by the Holy Spirit was incarnate of the Virgin Mary and became man.

For our sake he was crucified under Pontius Pilate, he suffered death and was buried, and rose again on the third day in accordance with the Scriptures. He ascended into heaven and is seated at the right hand of the Father. He will come again in glory to judge the living and the dead and his kingdom will have no end. I believe in the Holy Spirit, the Lord, the giver of life, who proceeds from the Father and the Son, who with the Father and the Son is adored and glorified, who has spoken through the prophets.

I believe in one, holy, Catholic and apostolic Church. I confess one Baptism for the forgiveness of sins, and I look forward to the resurrection of the dead and the life of the world to come.
Amen

A Prayer to Christ the King

O Lord our God, You alone are the Most Holy King and Ruler of all nations.

We pray to You, Lord, in the great expectation of receiving from You, O Divine King, mercy, peace, justice and all good things.

Protect, O Lord our King, our families and the land of our birth. Guard us we pray Most Faithful One.

Protect us from our enemies and from Your Just Judgment. Forgive us, O Sovereign King, our sins against you.

Jesus, You are a King of Mercy. We have deserved Your Just Judgment

Have mercy on us, Lord, and forgive us. We trust in Your Great Mercy.

O most awe-inspiring King, we bow before You and pray; May Your Reign, Your Kingdom, be recognized on earth. Amen

Prayer for Purification

Jesus, pour Thy Precious Blood over me, my body, mind, soul, and spirit; my conscious and sub-conscious; my intellect and will; my feelings, thoughts, emotions and passions; my words and actions; my vocation, my relationships, family, friends and possessions. Protect with Thy Precious Blood all other activities of my life. Lord I dedicate all of these things to Thee, and I acknowledge Thee as Lord and Master of all.

Mary, Immaculate Conception, pure and holy Virgin Mother of Our Lord Jesus Christ, draw each of us under Thy veil; guard me and shield me against all attacks and temptations that would violate the virtue of chastity.

Lord Jesus Christ, I beg Thee for the grace to remain guarded beneath the protective mantle of Mary, surrounded by the holy briar from which was taken the Holy Crown of Thorns, and saturated with Thy Precious Blood in the power of the Holy Spirit, with our Guardian Angels for the greater glory of the Father. Amen

Prayer for Pope

Almighty and everlasting God have mercy upon Thy servant, Pope, our Supreme Pontiff, and direct him, according to Thy loving kindness, in the way of eternal salvation; that, of Thy gift, he may ever desire that which is pleasing unto Thee and may accomplish it with all his might. Through Christ Our Lord. Amen.

Prayer for the Sick

Almighty and Eternal God, the everlasting salvation of them that believe, hear us on behalf of Thy sick servant, Name., for whom we implore the aid of Thy pitying mercy, that, with his/her bodily health restored, she/he may render thanks to Thee in Thy Church. Through Christ our Lord. Amen.

Prayer to Blessed Joseph by Pope Francis

Hail, Guardian of the Redeemer, Spouse of the Blessed Virgin Mary. To you God entrusted his only Son; in you Mary placed her trust; with you Christ became man. Blessed Joseph, to us too, show yourself a father and guide us in the path of life. Obtain for us grace, mercy and courage, and defend us from every evil. Amen

Prayer for the souls in Purgatory

"O Lord, who art ever merciful and bounteous with Thy gifts, look down upon the suffering souls in purgatory. Remember not their offenses and negligence's, but be mindful of Thy loving mercy, which is from all eternity. Cleanse them of their sins and fulfil their ardent desires that they may be made worthy to behold Thee face to face in Thy glory. May they soon be united with Thee and hear those blessed words which will call them to their heavenly home: "Come, blessed of My Father, take possession of the kingdom prepared for you from the foundation of the world."

Amen

Prayer Against Every Evil

Spirit of our God, Father, Son, and Holy Spirit, Most Holy Trinity, Immaculate Virgin Mary, angels, archangels, and saints of heaven, descend upon me. Please purify me, Lord, mould me, fill me with yourself, use me.

Banish all the forces of evil from me, destroy them, vanish them, so that I can be healthy and do good deeds.

Banish from me all spells, witchcraft, black magic, malefice, ties, maledictions, and the evil eye; diabolic infestations, oppressions, possessions; all that is evil and sinful, jealously, perfidy, envy; physical, psychological, moral, spiritual, diabolical aliments.

Burn all these evils in hell, that they may never again touch me or any other creature in the entire world.

I command and bid all the power who molest me – by the power of God all powerful, in the name of Jesus Christ our Saviour, through the intercession of the Immaculate Virgin Mary – to leave me forever, and to be consigned into the everlasting hell, where they will be bound by Saint Michael the archangel, Saint Gabriel, Saint Raphael, our guardian angels, and where they will be crushed under the heel of the Immaculate Virgin Mary.

Amen.

Prayer to Saint Benedict for Protection

O glorious St. Benedict, sublime model of all virtues, pure vessel of God's grace! Behold me, humbly kneeling at thy feet. I implore thy loving heart to pray for me before the throne of God.

To thee I have recourse in all the dangers which daily surround me. Shield me against my enemies, inspire me to imitate thee in all things. May thy blessing be with me always, so that I may shun whatever God forbids and avoid the occasions of sin.

Graciously obtain for me from God those favours and graces of which I stand so much in need, in the trials, miseries and afflictions of life. Thy heart was always so full of love, compassion, and mercy towards those who were afflicted or troubled in any way. Thou didst never dismiss without consolation and assistance anyone who had recourse to thee.

I therefore invoke thy powerful intercession, in the confident hope that thou wilt hear my prayers and obtain for me the special grace and favour I so earnestly implore (mention it), if it be for the greater glory of God and the welfare of my soul. Help me, O great St. Benedict, to live and die as a faithful child of God, to be ever submissive to His holy will, and to attain the eternal happiness of heaven. Amen.

Prayer to Saint Michael the Archangel

Saint Michael the Archangel, defend us in battle. Be our protection against the wickedness and snares of the devil. May God rebuke him we humbly pray; and do Thou, O Prince of the Heavenly Host, by the Power of God, cast into hell Satan and all the evil spirits, who prowl through the world seeking the ruin of souls. Amen.

Prayer to Saint Raphael the Archangel

Saint Raphael, the Archangel, arrow and medicine of Divine Love, wound our hearts, we implore you, with the burning love of God and let this wound never heal, so that even in daily life we might always remain upon the path of love and overcome all things through love. Amen.

Prayer to Saint Gabriel the Archangel

Blessed Saint Gabriel, Archangel We beseech you to intercede for us at the throne of divine mercy: As you announced the mystery of the Incarnation to Mary, so through your prayers may we receive strength of faith and courage of spirit, and thus find favour with God and redemption through Christ Our Lord. May we sing the praise of God our Saviour with the angels and saints in heaven forever and ever. Amen.

Prayer to Guardian Angel

O angel of God, my guardian dear to whom God's love commits me here. Ever this day/night be at my side to light, to guard, to rule and guide. Amen

Rosary

Rosary

The Rosary is a prayer. Pope Pius V in 1569 established a standard 15 Mysteries of the Rosary, based on long tradition of using beads or knots to count prayers. Knotted prayer ropes became popular in the 3rd century, so did doing Marian prayers. The fourth Mysteries were added in 2002 by Pope John Paul II. You should aim to do one rosary a day if possible, you can stop and start your rosary at any time. Many Popes, Saints and others, have spoken and written of the rosary's great prayer qualities.

How to pray the Rosary, start by making the Sign of the Cross.

Then say the Apostles' Creed.

Say the Our Father.

Say three Hail Marys.

Say the Glory Be.

Announce the First Mystery

Say the Our Father.

Say ten Hail Marys while meditating on the mystery.

Say the Glory Be.

Say the Fatima Prayer.

Announce the Second Mystery

Say the Our Father,

Say ten Hail Marys while meditating on the mystery.

Say the Glory Be.

Say the Fatima Prayer.

continue with Third, Fourth and Fifth Mysteries in the same manner.

Say the Hail Holy Queen.

Say prayer after rosary.

Finished

Apostles Creed

I believe in God, the Father almighty, Creator of heaven and earth, and in Jesus Christ, his only Son, our Lord, who was conceived by the Holy Spirit, born of the Virgin Mary, suffered under Pontius Pilate, was crucified, died and was buried; he descended into hell; on the third day he rose again from the dead; he ascended into heaven, and is seated at the right hand of God the Father almighty; from there he will come to judge the living and the dead. I believe in the Holy Spirit, the holy catholic Church, the communion of saints, the forgiveness of sins, the resurrection of the body, and life everlasting.

Amen

Our Father

Our Father, who art in heaven, hallowed be thy name. Thy kingdom come, thy will be done, on earth, as it is in heaven. Give us this day our daily bread and forgive us our trespasses as we forgive those who trespass against us; and lead us not into temptation, but deliver us from evil.

Amen

Hail Mary

Hail Mary, full of grace, the Lord is with you. Blessed are you among women, and blessed is the fruit of your womb, Jesus. Holy Mary, Mother of God, pray for us sinners, now and at the hour of our death. Amen

Glory Be

Glory be to the Father, and to the Son, and to the Holy Spirit. As it was in the beginning, is now, and ever shall be, world without end. Amen

Fatima Prayer

O my Jesus, forgive us our sins, save us from the fires of hell and lead all souls to heaven, especially those most in need of Thy mercy.

Hail Holy Queen

Hail! Holy Queen, Mother of Mercy, our life, our sweetness and our hope. To you do we cry, poor banished children of Eve. To you do we send our sighs, mourning and weeping in this valley of tears. Turn then, O most gracious advocate, your eyes of mercy toward us; and after this our exile show unto us the blessed fruit of your womb, Jesus.

O clement, O loving, O sweet virgin Mary. Pray for us, O Holy Mother of God, that we may be made worthy of the promises of Christ. Amen

Prayer after Rosary

O God whose only begotten Son by his life, death, and Resurrection has purchased for us the rewards of eternal life; grant we beseech thee, that meditating on these mysteries of the Most Holy Rosary of the Blessed Virgin Mary, we may imitate what they contain and obtain what they promise through the same Christ our Lord.

Amen

The Mysteries

Mysteries of the Rosary

There are traditionally Three sets of Mysteries, which are called Joyful, Sorrowful, Glorious, each having five parts. Joyful on Monday and Thursday, Sorrowful on Tuesday and Friday and Glorious on Wednesdays and Saturdays.

Sunday's Mysteries change, From the first Sunday of Advent until Lent it is included in the Joyful Mysteries. Then during the Sundays of Lent it is included in the Sorrowful Mysteries. And from Easter until Advent it is included in the Glorious Mysteries. The other days are fixed to the same Mysteries.

Joyful on Monday and Thursday.

1st Joyful Mystery, The Annunciation (Lk 1:26-38)

2nd Joyful Mystery, The Visitation (Lk 1:39-45)

3rd Joyful Mystery, The Birth of Jesus (Lk 2:1-14)

4th Joyful Mystery, The Presentation (Lk 2:22-38)

5th Joyful Mystery, Finding the Child Jesus in the Temple (Lk 2:41-52)

Sorrowful on Tuesday and Friday.

1st Sorrowful Mystery, Agony in the Garden (Mt 26:36-46)

2nd Sorrowful Mystery, Scourging at the Pillar (Jn 19:1-6)

3rd Sorrowful Mystery, Crowning with Thorns (Mt 27:27-31

4th Sorrowful Mystery, Carrying of the Cross (Mt 27:31-34)

5th Sorrowful Mystery, The Crucifixion (Jn 19:18-37)

Glorious on Wednesday and Saturday.

1st Glorious Mystery, The Resurrection (Lk 24:1-12)

2nd Glorious Mystery, The Ascension (Mk 16:19)

3rd Glorious Mystery, Descent of Holy Spirit (Acts 2:1-5)

4th Glorious Mystery, The Assumption (Lk 1:46-49)

5th Glorious Mystery, Coronation of the Blessed Virgin Mary (Rev 12:1)

The fourth Mystery is Luminous (of light) and is not always included as it was a later addition to the Mysteries (2002). If you want to include it, it does change the order of the Rosary. Luminous is on Thursdays, Joyful on Monday and Saturday, Glorious Mysteries on Wednesday and Sunday, Sorrowful Mysteries on Tuesday and Friday. With then Sundays of Advent and Christmas being Joyful, Sundays of Lent being Sorrowful, Other Sundays being Glorious.

Luminous on Thursdays.

1st Luminous Mystery, Baptism of Jesus (Mt 3:16-17)

2nd Luminous Mystery, Wedding at Cana (Jn 2:1-11)

3rd Luminous Mystery, Proclaiming the Kingdom (Mt 4: 12-17)

4th Luminous Mystery, Transfiguration of Jesus (Lk 9:30-35)

5th Luminous Mystery, Institution of the Eucharist (Mt 26:26-30)

Conclusion

Conclusion

Thank you for reading this book. I am not a great wordsmith or a master of grammar as you have read. I hope this book helps you understand your own beliefs better or that of your Catholic neighbours. There of course is a lot more to learn in becoming a Catholic, expanding your knowledge of the faith or in understanding Catholics and the Holy Catholic church. I hope to write more books in the very near future, hopefully another version of this book, which will go into more detail and hopefully will answer more questions Than this quick and simple book could possibly do. Please consider the reading list as a source of information.

Reading list

Reading List

Disinformation: Former Spy Chief Reveals Secret Strategies for Undermining Freedom, Attacking Religion, and Promoting Terrorism. By Ion Mihai Pacepa and Ronald J. Rychlak.

Infiltration: The Plot to Destroy the Church from Within. By Dr Taylor R. Marshall.

AA-1025: Memoirs of a communist's infiltration into the Church. By Marie Carre.

The Myth of Hitler's Pope: How Pope Pius XII Rescued Jews from the Nazis. By Rabbi David G. Dalin.

Can a Catholic Be a Socialist? By Trent Horn and Catherine Ruth Pakaluk.

The Case For Patriarchy. Timothy J. Gordon.

Apologetics and Catholic Doctrine. Archbishop Michael Sheehan and Fr Peter Joseph.

Hard Sayings: A Catholic approach to answering Bible difficulties. By Trent Horn.

20 Answers Series: Faith & Science. By Catholic Answers.

Why We're Catholic: Our reasons for Faith, Hope and Love. By Trent Horn.

Love Unleashes Life: Abortion and the act of communicating Truth. Stephanie Gray Connors.

Pope Paul VI On Human Life: Humanae Vitae. By Mary Eberstadt, James Hitchcock, and Jennifer Fulwiler.

Magisterial Authority. By FR Chad Ripperger, PHD.

History of Christendom Volume 1 to 6, by Warren H. Carroll.

Bearing False Witness, Debunking Centuries Of Anti-Catholic History, Rodney Stark.

Counterfeit Spirituality, Exposing the False Gods, Bryan Mercier.

The Life of Christ, Fulton J. Sheen.

A Pocket Guide to Catholic Apologetics, Patrick Madrid.

Where is that in the Bible?, Patrick Madrid.

Ask your Husband: A Wife's Guide to True Femininity, Mrs Timothy J Gordon.

The Early Church Was the Catholic Church, Joe Heschmeyer.

The Church and the Roman Empire (301–490), Reclaiming Catholic History. Mike Aquilina.

Start with What: 10 Principles for Thinking about Assisted Suicide, Stephanie Gray Connors.

Mr Good Enough: The case for choosing a Real Man over holding out for Mr Perfect, Lori Gottlieb.

Daily Defense: 365 Days Plus O: 365 Days Plus One to Becoming a Better Apologist, Jimmy Akin.

Are Canonizations Infallible?: Revisiting a Disputed Question, multiple authors.

Catholic Bible Dictionary, Scott Hahn.

The Didache.

The standard Catholic Edition Bible (non-Catholic Bibles are not from God but from the minds of men.)

The Catechism of Trent, Baltimore and The Penny Catechism.

olrfamilycatechism.com (Baltimore)

thecatholictruth.org (Website/YouTube)

www.catholic.com (Catholic answers)

The Counsel of Trent (YouTube channel)

Fr. Matt Hartley, YouTube

www.citadelpublishing.co.uk

Final Note

Humanity was created, then lost.

Christ came and died for us.

He gave the Faith to St Peter, St Peter built Christ's church, the Catholic church.

It formed the pillars of the Faith, it was given the Bible.

Heresies sprung from the darkness clawing into men's hearts, turning them against Christ and his only Church, one after another, they came.

The enemies of salvation are many.

We are few, but our Faith is strong, its power is undeniable.

It is TRUTH.

It is JUSTICE.

It is LOVE.

It is LAW.

It is SALVATION.

We have stood our ground for millennia, we are never ending, never broken, we do not falter, we ask for nothing but to serve God.

The world knows no faith, no mercy, it offers no salvation, only damnation.

God and his Church, offers us, Everything.

Heretics once again assault us from all sides.

Hear me Brothers and Sisters, We need the Church.

Fight against the devil and all his allies. Refuse Heresy in all its forms.

Or separate yourself from God and his Church and be cast into the pit.

Do not abandon hope, your soul is eternal, we are eternal.

Love God.

Fight until you see Heaven.

GOD WILLS IT

Printed in Great Britain
by Amazon

26813834R00066